Mostly

Paul Hostovsky

FUTURECYCLE PRESS

www.futurecycle.org

Cover artwork by Stanislav Veselý; author photo by Marlene Hostovsky; cover and interior book design by Diane Kistner; Georgia text and Caliban titling

Library of Congress Control Number: 2021934677

Published by FutureCycle Press
Athens, Georgia, USA

ISBN 978-1-952593-17-8

For Marlene

Contents

I.

II.

III.

IV.

Donc, voilà, c'est un poème, et bien, what next?

—Mark Halliday

What we're mostly faced with are these privacies,
inconsequential to all but us.

—Stephen Dunn

I know I know I know I know I know I know

—Paul Simon

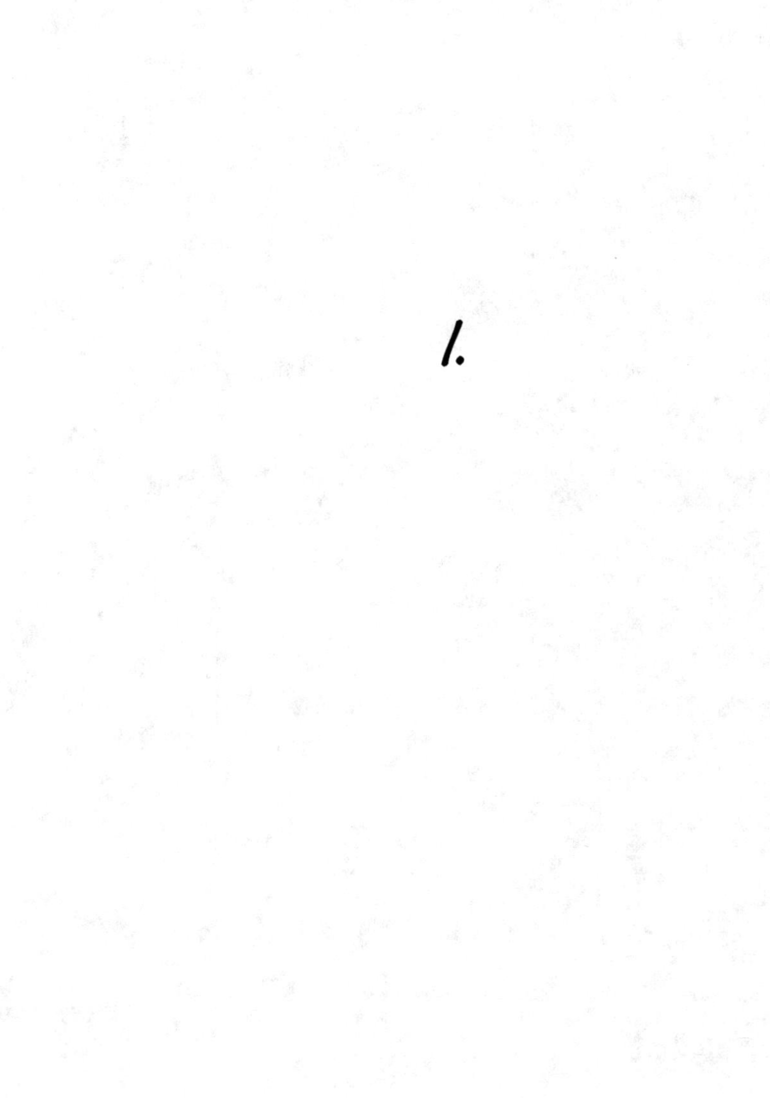

1.

Love Letter to Carl Sandburg

I'm sipping my tea on the ground floor
of the Federal Reserve Building,
a handful of suits at the table behind me
talking about profit margins, inventories,
low-hanging fruit, when I notice this little girl
on the sidewalk outside the window,
conducting the wind with her tiny hands,
the autumn wind, which is counting its money
and throwing it away, counting its money
and throwing it away—a whirlwind of dancing leaves
going up and around and around in the wind tunnel
that this tall building I'm sitting in has created
with the other tall buildings. And as though
she had created it, she conducts it, shapes it,
urges it with her twirling hands
to keep counting its money and throwing it away,
counting its money and throwing it away
in front of the Federal Reserve, where now I see
her mother waiting at the curb with a big
suitcase and a little suitcase, texting,
scanning the intersection for their ride-share,
not looking at the girl or the swirling leaves,
looking only at her phone and the endless line of cars,
searching for the one that's theirs. And when it pulls up
on the opposite side of Atlantic Avenue,
she waves to the girl to come—now—hurry!
And the girl waves goodbye to the symphony of leaves
that goes on playing and dancing without her
as she pulls the little suitcase behind the mother
who is pulling the big suitcase toward the waiting car.
And I can almost feel you here, right beside me,
seeing what I'm seeing, wanting what I'm wanting:
to write it all down, not for the suits at the table behind us,
still talking about expenditures and revenues,
but for the wind that goes on counting its money
and throwing it away on Atlantic Avenue.

Going Back

It's not that I want to be young again—
God no. I wouldn't wish that on my worsted-
sweatered-old-man-in-sensible-shoes
self. I mean, we barely made it out alive
the first time around. But I'd like to talk to him—
that lonely, bored, back-row kid
I was back then. Because I think he would have
liked me. I mean, I think he would have liked
the way he turned out. And I know he would have liked
to ask me a million questions. Many of which
I know the answers to. I picture us sitting
on a bench in Taylor Park, one of his PF Fliers
jackhammering nervously next to my sensible shoes.
He looks away. Doesn't speak. I ask him if
there's anything he'd like to know. He looks up at me—
from this angle he can see all my ugly nose hairs,
thick as grave-grass. I no longer even bother
to trim them. "How old are you?" he asks me,
and I tell him: 62. "Do you have any kids?" Yes. Two.
"Where are they now?" One is in New York City
and one is in Hawaii. "Do you miss them?"
Yes. Very much. But I miss you even more,
if that's possible. "Am I going to beat Marc Peo
in the wrestling tournament?" Now it's my turn
to look away. "That's OK," he says, "you don't
have to say it. I understand." And he puts his little hand
on my shoulder. "What about Cheryl Lubecki?"
What *about* her? "Well, do you think she likes me?"
I think your strategy of pretending not to be interested in her
isn't working. "OK, thanks for telling me." And he looks
away again. A long silence. The trees in the park,
which are much older than both of us, seem to chortle
in the breeze. Is there anything else you'd like to know?
He takes a minute to think. Then asks, "Are you happy?"
Oh yes, in fact (and I start to choke up a little) being here now
with you, I am happier than I have ever been in my life.

Wording

Every poem should have a bird in it
—Mary Oliver

Cynosure, gravid, pabulum—
just three of the many
unusual specimens
I'd been lucky enough to glimpse
in the last few days.
And then at the dentist
I heard *risible* singing
from behind my hygienist's
face mask: "These muscles
around your mouth," she said,
"are your risible muscles,"
and I reached for my metaphorical
binoculars and feasted
on *risible* perched at the edge
of that noun phrase,
where I'd never seen it before.
It was a rare sighting and I could sense
the dinosaur DNA of that dactyl
going all the way back to the Old French *rire,*
and the Latin *ridere,* and maybe
I felt a little *ridiculous*
as I offered her my invisible
binoculars and she declined because
she was wearing a face shield
over her face mask, and her hands were full
of my teeth. Nevertheless, I know she appreciated
risible the way I appreciated it
when I heard its song—which sounds like
laughter—emanating from her own mouth
as I sat there with my mouth open
wider than song, wider than laughter,
as wide as a baby-bird mouth.

Indolent

"If you're going to get cancer,
this is the one to get,"
said my radiation oncologist.
"It isn't the aggressive kind.
It's what they call the indolent kind.
Hell, you'll probably get hit by a bus
before you die of this thing."
And he looked out the window.
And I looked out the window.
There was a bus stop
across the street. But there wasn't
a bus. And there were no people waiting
for the bus. Nevertheless, it was a bus stop
the way the cancer was a cancer. It was
official. You could look it up
on the transit authority's list of city bus stops
and there it would be: #39 on the corner
of Walnut and Peabody. You could
go to radiation oncology and there
I would be: 51 with my cancer, the one
to get, the indolent kind that misses
the doctor's appointment
because it missed the #39 bus
because it couldn't get out of bed this morning
because it was having such a wonderful dream,
a flying dream in which, amazingly,
just by doing nothing,
by remaining absolutely still,
suddenly you're flying.

Hold at the Circulation Desk

He returned the book, which was late,
and would have paid the benign

library fine, but the librarian's heart,
which was beating sixty to a hundred

times per minute (but who's
counting), sending blood to her face

and hands, carrying the rich oxygen
through her magnificent circulatory system

to every cell in her body,
was an open, generous heart:

"It's three days late but, hey, who's
counting?" she said in a sweetly singing

exoneration. Then she handed him his hold,
which had traveled all those arteries

and roadways from some faraway
circulation desk to her circulation desk,

and while she was checking him out
he checked her out, discreetly bookmarking

her slightly parted lips, reader's hands, perfectly
turned shoulders as she handed him back

his library card and smiled a bookish smile
that he held in his heart as he left the library

with his hold. He read it quickly,
returned it early.

What Happens When You Die

is someone has to pronounce
your death, which is, of course,
unpronounceable. There are no words
for this. And yet we say
death. We used to say *deeth*
in Middle English, and before that, *Tod*
in Old High German (the final *d*
properly pronounced like a *t*).
It's called The Pronouncement of Death
form, and someone has to fill it out.
And it can't be just anyone. It has to be
a physician, someone who ostensibly
knows how to pronounce the name
of the thing that killed you, and presumably
knows its etiology, though probably not the etymology
of *death*. And there's a good
possibility he won't pronounce
your name right, especially if your name
is Hostovsky, which people are always
mispronouncing and misspelling, even though
it's properly pronounced exactly the way
it's written. Anyway, now that you're dead,
it is given to him to pronounce it. And then
there are lots of other forms to be filled out.
There is the death certificate and the cremation form
and the union and pension forms
and the social security form and the bank account
reconciliation form, and so on and so forth. And so
there will be the sound of writing, a sound you loved well
when you lived and wrote. That productive sound
of putting pen to paper—there will be a lot of that
when you die. And even though it's not
the kind of writing you would choose if it were
up to you, still, it is writing. And in that,
if nothing else, you can take some solace.

Sneeze

I love the benign
violence of it—
impossible
not to close your eyes
when this small
homemade bomb goes off,
unnerving
a few bystanders,
but causing no
injury or damage,
and then—incoming!—
a second explosion,
and maybe a third,
then a rickety lull—
itchy, intoxicating—
before the final
salvo, finale, sonic
boom! Clean
sweep. Mission
accomplished.
Knowing smiles
and blessings all around.
No need for alarm,
no return fire, no
casualties, no grieving.
Just clearing
the old nasal mucosa
of all the latest
foreign invaders,
thank you very much.

Grr

I love the grouchy words—
peevish, irascible, fractious—
I am all of them—crabby, morose,
snarky and more. I hate the phrase
"and more." It's so American, so
manifest destiny. I hate all the increase,
all the excess, all the productivity—
the abundance, the stuff, the shelves
upon shelves. And the free
shipping. We're prolific as fuck, and I am
such an asshole. I'm surly, tetchy,
moody, nasty and gnarly. I admit it.
I revel in it. I'm querulous, captious,
and vindictive. And it's not just the adjectives I love.
I love the verbs, too. Lour, glower,
growl and glare. And snarl. And more!
My stepdaughter gave me a T-shirt
with Grumpy on it. You know, Grumpy
of Seven Dwarves' fame? I love it.
I own it. I wear it like a badge of
assholiness. Like a bellying flag. Listen,
don't be an asshole if you can help it.
But if you can't help it, help
others to understand the assholes.
Be an ambassador of assholes.
Wear it on your sleeve, on your chest,
on your boobs. Wear it on your belly.
Because you can't be what you want to be if
you can't be what you are first. So go ahead,
be that way. And if you don't love yourself,
try loving the superabundance of pithy words
for describing someone as hateful as you.

Vernal Scrooge

The hounds of spring are on winter's traces and I hate
a slobbering dog. All this mucus and affection
is making me sick, not to mention the ejaculations
of the junipers, oaks, alders and maples—I can't
stop sneezing and I'm all congested. The erectile
tail feathers of the wild turkeys—the way the males
display them proudly to the females—leave the females
unimpressed. I, too, am unimpressed with spring
and all its fecundity. I miss the white lie
of the noiseless, atoning snow; the brown study
of the bare, ramifying trees; the long, cold, invisible
diapause of the insects. I hate to be a buzzkill, but
the bees aren't disappearing fast enough for me.
All these propagators and multipliers—the springtails
dropping their sperm on the ground and just waiting
for the females to come and pick it up—they can all
go fuck themselves. You can all go fuck yourselves,
you lovers of spring, you gardeners and joggers
and dogwood-huggers. I say there's too much sex
in the world, too much fruitfulness, too much seed
on the wind, too much pollen in the air, and much
too much begetting on the ground. I'm getting too old
for this. I'm staying in and counting the days till fall.

Talent

He played that thing all the time: waking, sleeping, walking, riding his bike, reclining in the bathtub fully clothed—where the acoustics were the best, he said. And in the backseat of the family Buick when we were trying to have a conversation up front. It was annoying. If we turned the radio on to shut him up, he simply played along with it, the squeaky little shit. It never occurred to us that he was on his way to greatness. One of the greatest harmonica players ever: jazz, folk, rock, Latin, blues, country, even classical. The inventor of the chromatic playing style on a regular diatonic ten-hole harmonica. But to us he was just the kid who sucked and blew and drooled a lot with that thing forever installed in his mouth, alternately buzzing like a beard of bees, chugging like a locomotive, wailing like a professional mourner, chiming like a bell, whistling like a blue jay or a catcall, squeezing out the chords and major triads like an accordion, then bending one single note so low, so lonely, that it almost broke. Mom lost it once, screaming "Put that thing away! I can't hear"—she was on the phone—and she confiscated all of them (he had one for every key) for a whole week. He wept and begged her to give them back—"just one, please, I'll play quietly"—but she wouldn't relent. He cried and cried, emitting these strange low animal noises and high keening sounds as though he had a blues harmonica stuck somewhere deep down inside him and was trying to get it out. She hid them in the fruit bowl, under the apples, which she knew he never ate. I reached for an apple, glimpsed the shining underneath, the buried treasure he'd have killed for and was dying without.

Anonymity

Remember that alcoholic you tried to help, the one you took to those meetings, those meetings you were attending yourself because you needed help stopping drinking and the only way to get it, they said at the meetings, was to give it? Remember those boxes he asked if he could store in your garage because he'd just lost his apartment and was basically homeless now? Remember how you made a place for them in a dry corner near the bicycles and Christmas decorations? Remember how he promised he'd come back for them soon, but then he stopped coming to the meetings and months went by and soon it was winter, the boxes huddled in the dark against the cold? Remember how you made it through the holidays without a drink, then asked around at the meetings but no one had seen him? Remember how you thought of looking online for an obituary but you didn't even know his last name—because anonymity, they said at the meetings, was the spiritual foundation of all their traditions? Remember when you decided to open the boxes—just to look for his name, you told yourself—and (Merry Christmas!) what you found were hundreds of albums and CDs: oldies rock and jazz and folk and blues, many of them rare and out of print? Remember how you carried them into the house and took them out one by one and made a list of the titles and listened to all of them over the next sober weeks and months and by the time you celebrated a year clean and sober his record collection had merged with your record collection? And someone at the meetings said he was dead. "Are you sure?" you asked. "Yeah, they found him frozen to death last Christmas in a snowbank." Remember the brief shock, then the sweet relief you felt wash over you, thinking only of the records and yourself? Remember how that sweetness turned sour, how it started to burn, how you couldn't listen to the records anymore, the pleasure gone now? Remember how you ended up selling them all for a thousand bucks, then ended up picking up a drink, then ended up spending the money on booze and drugs, then ended up back at the meetings, where the help was, the help you got by giving it away?

Barbershop

"Nobody calls it a barbershop anymore
except you, Dad," says my son
when I tell him that's where we're going.
It seems it's called Cost Cutters. And they're called
hairstylists. It isn't even called
a haircut anymore—it's called a taper, or a fade,
or a number two on top and a number
one on the sides. And there isn't
a coke machine by the door anymore
that sells coke in glass bottles. There isn't
a transistor radio up on a shelf anymore
with the ballgame on. There isn't
a red-and-white-striped barber's pole outside Dominic's
with an old Italian barber named Dominic—
who's been there all my life and probably
most of his life—pushing the long broom
a little closer to my mother, flirting with her,
anymore. But some things haven't changed: They still
wrap you in a cape, and they still
look at you looking back at them in the mirror
as they stand behind you and ask you
what you want. And what you want,
though they call it something else now,
hasn't changed either: They still touch you
in a way that feels good, and they make you look good
and smell good, too, and you still walk out of there
feeling a little lighter, a little younger, a little closer
to beauty, though nobody calls it that because you're a boy.

Song of the Only Childhood

Matthew Cook played the oboe.
Billy Most's mother's name was Myrna.
Rita Demezzo lived across the street
when I was twelve. These are just three
of the countless useless factoids from my only
childhood, which I don't know what to do with
except write them down here. Mrs. Schachtel
gave out candied apples on Halloween.
Andrea Inguaggiato played the bassoon.
Howard Lafferty had a lisp. Craig Carey
had a flouncy way of walking. I want to
list them all here, like the catalog of ships
in the Iliad, the "begats" in the Bible, the loves
of Whitman in Whitman. I loved Faith Roffman,
but she loved Mark Winkles. David Needleman
played the clarinet. I wrestled Marc Peo
in junior high and lost. Cary Heller was left-
handed but he could switch-hit. My only childhood
disappeared like a long fly ball that went sailing
over the fence, over the houses, over the treetops—
a long fly ball, flying. The lady on Oval Road
gave out No. 2 pencils on Halloween. Richard Singer
threw like a girl. Andy Tessler changed his name
to Andy Freedman. But we still called him Tessler.
Michael Canson's mother's name was Zelda.
His father's name was Myron. They grounded
Canson for life and I never saw him again. Stephen
Shapiro played timpani. I played trombone. My mother's
name was Regina. My father's name was Egon,
pronounced *Egg*-on. He grew up in Czechoslovakia
and didn't speak English all that well. He thought
a home run was something you did when your mother
forgot to pick you up after your baseball game.

To a Toddler Bawling in a Stroller

I don't wanna,
either.
You're right,
the world is hideous—
one can only
weep. I wanna
scream my head off
next to your
screaming head, our red
faces contorting
in concert,
the people passing by
all joining in
irresistibly,
wailing and keening
in chorus,
with you the lead
crooner,
bandleader,
maestro.

Omission

What I didn't tell you about
was the forgotten
long-expired bag of lettuce
all the way in the back
looking bloodshot,
asphyxiated,
tragic as a traffic
accident under plastic,
that I came across
in search of the Lombardy
olives and goat cheese—
and how, making a face,
I gingerly extracted
the sodden, sealed,
severed heads of Romaine
from behind the chilling
horizontal bottle of Chardonnay,
tossed them into the bin
with a dead-sounding thud,
then washed my hands of them
before returning for the wine
and cheese and olives,
serving them up to you without
a word of what I'd seen.

Knowledge

It's good to know
there's a part of me
I don't know
that knows.

It knows where
I came from,
and it knows where
I will go.

It's not the part
they say God
loved into being,
the part they call
the soul.

It's the part that
used to love
climbing trees
and still loves

gazing at them,
as if that's where
I will go
when the time comes.
The way our old

Labrador seemed to know
and walked off
into the woods
to die there alone.

I don't know
how to die.
But I don't
need to know

because it knows.

II.

Elegy

for all the
skinny
lovely
wistful
brilliant
brave
unread
poetry
collections
out there
with their
spines
leaning
left or
right or
maybe
posture
perfectly
straight
like our own
beloved
children
standing
at attention
chin up
chest out
name tag
showing
or else
horizontal
piled
supine
like the dead
like so
much dust
collecting
dust

Trump Inaugural Poem

"FUCK YOU" is a spondee.
"FUCK you," with the stress
on the first syllable, is a trochee
whose rejoinder is either
an iamb ("Fuck YOU")
or an anapest ("No, fuck YOU").
Poetic meter and poetic devices
are not only not boring, they're
basic as breath, relevant
as politics or sex. "The dick
in the White House is not my
president" is a good example
of synecdoche—that part of him
representing the whole of him,
who does not represent me,
who does not represent anyone
I know, who does not represent
anything I believe in—which is
not only a fact, a true fact, but also
a beautiful example of anaphora.

Fan Letter

I love. Your book. Your voice. The writing is so gorgeous, so limpid that I can see clear down to the beautiful muck, the beautiful darkness, which wasn't beautiful until the writing made it so. I would follow that voice anywhere, even into the darkness, keep it like a picture, like your picture on the back cover, your finger touching your cheek thoughtfully. I love. Thoughtfully. The darkness. I'm not some creep, OK? I was at the writers conference and I heard you read, and I said to myself: Holy shit! Holy shit, like I'm suddenly looking up at a mammoth full moon; like I'm stepping out into a sudden, violent downpour; like I just got to the end of a poem that knocked my socks off. Holy shit! I have to get her book. And your book is like a book that someone I loved loved. Like a book they lent me but I never read it or bothered to return it when we broke up and years went by with its spine leaning this way and that on my shelf like a stowaway among the jostling passengers with their bright jackets. Until one day. One day I opened the book. And I started reading. I sat down and kept on reading, shaking my head at just how fine the writing was and how could I have let so many years—and how many years had it been?—go by without ever opening this book, this book that someone I loved had loved. Because that's what the voice sounds like. And I read all day and late into the night. Until I finished it. And now I feel bereft because. Because I loved this book. I loved it. I love it. I love.

To the One Who Stole a Book at My Poetry Reading

Good writers borrow, great writers steal,
they say. I say it belonged to you already—
the sounds of the words, the spell of the words,
and the words themselves, they belong
to all of us. As do the silences. As does
the breath. Ours the air in the room, ours
the shared mouth where the words live,
ours the deepest listening. Listen, after
the reading, when they lined up to buy my book,
it felt a little like extortion: me taking their money
and giving them back what was already theirs.
Poetry belongs to everyone. And no one.
Kudos to you for insisting on that. Thank you
for reminding me my poems aren't my poems.

To the People Who Don't Write Back

Maybe you haven't written because
you're still reading
and re-reading what I sent you,
giving it the kind of close read it deserves,
the kind a lover gives a love letter,
a Sumerian scholar gives a cuneiform tablet,
a reader of poetry gives a poem she doesn't
totally get but can't get enough of.

Or maybe you haven't written because
you're still writing, still
agonizing over the right words,
deleting the superfluous poignancies,
rethinking the commas,
looking for better verbs, discarding
sentences, whole paragraphs, then starting
all over again. Then again,

maybe you haven't written because
people don't write anymore,
let alone read. Letter writing has gone the way of
candlelight. They're shouting "short-form copy"
from the rooftops and the laptops. The mailboxes
are disappearing. And so are all the letter writers.
And all the English majors. And the English language itself
is shrinking at the same time it's expanding—

not unlike the universe. Plus, the children
no longer collect stamps, nor even know
in which corner of the envelope to affix them.
Maybe you haven't written because
there is death in the world. And evil and email
in the universe. Maybe you're dead.
Or maybe I haven't heard from you because
I'm dead. And just don't know it yet.

That She's Beautiful

is beside the point.
What was the point
of his saying that she's beautiful
in the context of
her poem? I don't care
if he's a Bollingen
Prize winner with ten
collections under his belt—
what's under his belt
is the problem—you can't
say to someone they're beautiful
in an undergraduate poetry
workshop out of context, out of
the blue, even if it's
true. "Beauty is truth
and truth beauty" is bullshit—
it's sexual harassment,
is what it is. The way he looked at her
while praising her poem,
"its shape, its movement, its
passion," as though it were *her* shape
and *her* movement and *his*
passion—it grossed me out. The guy
could be her grandfather.
And the way he phrased it: "May I
just say, Clara, you are a very
beautiful woman," as though
it were a question—which it wasn't—
as though he were asking
permission to touch her breasts
while in the act of touching them,
then quoting Keats like that, it was
disingenuous and disgusting
is all I know, and all I need to know.

Resonance

Sometimes the poem resonates
and the people nod and sigh. They say
mmm. They hear you and they feel
less alone. And you feel less alone
because you've shared something
that belongs to everyone. But then
there are other times—and you never
know which it will be—when the poem
doesn't resonate. The lines about the pleasure
you derive from sniffing your own earwax
do not strike a chord. And all you hear
is silence. Crickets. You never felt
so alone. And what can you do but
scratch your head, scratch the lines,
scratch your ear and sniff your finger
for the residue you could have sworn
was redolent of something much deeper.

Luckier

Praise the man
who lives on the corner of 109 and Lake
and hasn't mowed his lawn
in years—
all those flowering weeds,
untamed shrubs,
hegemony of ivies
claiming that yard like
a promised land,
not to mention the grass
he has let grow so long
that the leaves—
the leaves of grass—
could hide the girth of a man
as large as Whitman
if he lay down there
and looked up at the clouds,
a blade of grass in his teeth.
I don't know who he is
but I know the neighbors
are calling his yard an eyesore,
they're calling it obscene—
the way Whitman,
the father of free verse,
was called obscene in his day
for his overt sensuality. But I say
praise the man with the sensual lawn,
the epic lawn going onward
and outward on the corner of Lake
and 109, praise his genius
for freedom, so American, so
ahead of its time, transcending
all the manicured, boxy work
of his unimaginative contemporaries.

Cat Poem

The cat cleaning itself,
like the poem about the cat cleaning itself,
is focused on one thing only:

one, two, three
and sometimes one, two, three, four
accented licks to the forepaw,
then a rub

to the ear, which is where
the true focus of all these diligent
dripping syllables lies,

the licking a kind of
calibrated flow from a faucet
onto a washcloth,

the softly repeating hook
to the ear a kind of chorus, a kind of
Q-Tip, a kind of hook
that has distracted you from your life,

from yourself, from your focus
on yourself, the way the cat
suddenly stops, looks up, ears shaped

like a hat changing heads
on its head, listening for something else
to focus on. And detecting
nothing out there more compelling

than this, it returns to it
and gives itself over to it
utterly.

Po Biz

I didn't care about money.
Probably because we had
money. The money was like
air, it was there, it was like
what's the big deal it's just
money? So I didn't think about
making money, I thought about making
poems. Great poems. I wanted
to be a starving poet. I aspired
to be an alcoholic writer. And an artist
in a life drawing class for the rest
of my life. Then I graduated

from that liberal arts college
my parents paid for, where I
learned how to drink liberally,
to write a kick-ass sonnet, to bed
all the nude models who read
poetry. But no one was hiring
poets. And the money was like
the diminishing air you breathe
and rebreathe in a paper bag
to keep from hyperventilating—
which doesn't work. It's a myth. Not
one of those great myths they teach

in college, where people turn into
trees, gods turn into people, heroes
wrestle with their tragic flaws—
the great myths the great poets
write about. No, a minor poet writes
about the minor myths: Breathe
into a paper bag. Use Krazy Glue
to seal small wounds. Send your poem
to twenty lit mags and one might
whisper its sweet acceptance in your ear
and give you lots of money for your one
and only first North American serial rights.

Poem at the Breakfast Place

The girl who rings me up at the breakfast place
is wearing a T-shirt that says BREAKFAST SANDWICH
in big letters across her chest. "How's the breakfast
sandwich?" I ask her, not looking at her breasts
because I am by nature a fearful and shy man
and because I like talking about things without naming them
the way you sometimes can in poems. "It's really good," she says,
and gives me a smile that says she doesn't
like poetry but likes this poem so far. "I would love
to have that breakfast sandwich every single morning
of my life," I tell her as I give her the money
for my Earl Grey tea and apple cruller. "Then you must change
your order," she says, misquoting the last line
of Rilke's "Archaic Torso of Apollo." I look down
at my cup, my cruller oozing apple, then furtively at her lovely young
torso. "Life!" I correct her as she hands me my change,
frowning at me now, not with displeasure but
concentration, like she's really trying to get this poem.

Recycled Sestina

It's hard to feel good about
single-stream recycling
and those enormous receptacles
with the name *Harvey* written on them
trundling up and down the highways going
who knows where—

They remind me of that sestina
about recycling, the one with my name on it
and *plastic, paper, glass, cardboard, aluminum, tin*
thrown together in a kind of calibrated jumble
in every stanza,

each recycled end-word coming up
again and again, like in a tumble dryer,
the whole thing revolving
around a single bad idea. It was garbage

and I never published it. But E. L. Harvey,
the waste management company with the big receptacles,
has other ideas. And *Harvey* is published on the broadside
of every truck in the fleet, all of them hauling around

the same big idea. I'm stuck here behind one now
in traffic going nowhere, thinking about
my poem. It all gets sent over to Asia, you know,
for processing. Then they send it back over here. Talk about

waste. Talk about pretense. I mean, that would be like me
throwing away my sestina, then translating it
into Chinese. Then rehashing it here and putting
my name on it. Then waving it around in your face
like it was something to feel good about.

Writing Assignment

A platitude and a platypus
have one thing in common:
their first syllable,
which comes from the Greek
for flat. The resemblance
ends there. Because a platitude,
which is sometimes referred to
as a cliché, is nothing like
a platypus, which is sometimes referred to
as the duck-billed platypus.
Bill of a duck, tail of a beaver, feet
of an otter, the platypus
is no platitude. It's an original—
the sole living representative
of its family and genus. Write
platypuses, undergraduates. Be
original, be surprising. Be the venomous
mammal that lays eggs, figuratively
speaking, whenever you write
or speak. Don't be flat or trite
like a platitude. Be the flat-footed
platypus with a body so genuine
that early European scientists
thought it was a fake—several
animals sewn together. Don't be all
you can be; be everything you aren't.
Be sphinxian and alive for once
in your life. One page. Due Friday at 5.

A Spiritual Experience

Clifford threw his back out
while sitting in his car
in traffic. "Don't tell anyone," he said
when I asked him how it happened.
"I won't," I said but I didn't say I wouldn't
write a poem about it. He'd had to pee
bad. And the traffic was going nowhere.
And he had an empty peanut butter jar
that he kept in the glove compartment
for just such occasions—this was not
his first time. He twisted it open, twisted
himself into position, and it was right there
in the twisting that he somehow ruptured
a disc. And where is the poem in all this?
you're probably wondering. It's here
in the movement, the passion, the sequence
of twists that a man maneuvering to pee
in a small space in a small cup
performs while seated, the terrible need
to relieve himself a kind of passion,
the holding it in a kind of compression,
the letting it go finally a kind of pleasure
that gives way to a kind of wisdom
that washes over and comforts the afflicted
Clifford. "But which came first," I asked him,
"the pain of the slipped disc or the pleasure
of the peeing?" I needed to know for my own sake
and the sake of the poem. "It was a merging,"
he said, "a conflation of pleasure and pain, sorrow
and joy." It was ultimately what you would call
a spiritual experience, Clifford penultimately moaning
with the epiphany of it, his cup running over.

Laughing in the Face of Fear

I'm too chicken
to laugh in the face of fear.
But after
the fear has passed
I've been known to laugh
at fear's back.
Like when it's behind me
and I'm looking back at it
sauntering off,
growing smaller and smaller
until it's so tiny
it's laughable. Like the time
I thought that lump
was a tumor, but it was just
a bug-bite.
Or the time I went to the urologist
who said it was just
the asparagus,
and I practically peed
from laughing so hard.
If I could only
make fear turn around
when I'm laughing at fear's
back like that,
then I'd be laughing
in the face of fear.
Or maybe that's just
wordplay. For some of us,
words are all we have, though,
finally. Scary thought.

Poem in Stone

(for Marea Gordett)

There's a poem written in stone
outside this Boston T stop
on the corner of Tremont and Oak,

a poem about the evanescence of flowers,
installed here permanently
as part of a larger, citywide effort

to get more poetry out there into the world,
where flowers and poems
have a hard time competing. It's a fine effort,

five unrhymed quatrains etched
into a slab of granite
rising from a plinth on the busy sidewalk,

where the people are passing by, not
reading the poem, not smelling the flowers.
It's spring in the poem but it's winter

in Boston. The concrete plinth is already
beginning to crumble above the frost heaves.
It just goes to show, not even stone

can save a poem. But sometimes
flowers can. Orange tiger lilies,
roses and the fragile

pink bleeding hearts.

Lost

I could do without the world.
Just give me a letter
about the world,
one that I could
fold up in a pocket
and carry around with me,
and take it out now and then,
and pore over it,
and weep over it,
tasting the salt tears
as I fold it up and put it away again—
a letter I've read so many times
I've memorized it
so I don't really need
the moist, creased, crumpled
disappearing thing itself
in my hands anymore
because it's in my head now.
And yet if I ever lost it
I'd be lost.

Good Book

Sometimes you can't *not* put the book down
to save it, savor it, smile and shake your head
at just how good the writing is
in certain places, just how fine
the choices are in the uncertain
ways, the beautiful lost ways
you trust a good writer to see you through—

can't *not* put the book down
to look up a word you don't know,
or a word you once knew but can't
quite place now, like a face you recognize
but can't say how you know the one it belongs to,
even as you find yourself falling
in love with that face, wanting to know it
through and through—

can't *not* put the book down
just to sigh, stretch, look up at the ceiling
and be in your body with the book closed
in your hand, your finger inside it holding your place,
the disappearing place where you've been losing
yourself—deliberately, deliciously, abstemiously.
Like very fine chocolate, just a little
at a time. Okay maybe a little more.

Slow Turtles

There should be a comma
after *Slow,* I think,
pausing

before the hand-painted sign
that someone has propped up
on the causeway

where I go for my walks
and where the cars go by
too fast,

putting the slow turtles
at risk, not to mention
the slow bipeds.

It's ambiguous
without the comma, I think.
But then I think: No,

it's perfect the way it is,
this unpunctuated
found poem

giving the reader—
the motorist, the bicyclist,
the pedestrian—

pause.

Birches

He chip-carved the words
into a small piece of basswood—
Susan, will you marry me?—
then took the carving to the arboretum,
where he chose a white birch
because he loved the Frost poem—
Earth's the right place for love—
and the symbolism: the white
papery bark like a wedding dress
peeling off against his cheek
as he shinnied up the trunk to the upper
branches and nailed it there
high up in the tree.
                That evening,
he told her about the starling migrations,
hundreds of thousands of birds
like a river in the sky (that part was
true), and "they'll be here tomorrow" (that part
he invented). "Let's go birdwatching
in the arboretum and see what we
can see." She didn't suspect a thing.
He packed the ring, a small bottle
of champagne, two plastic flutes,
a picnic blanket, bird book, pair of binoculars.
                They spread the blanket out
on a grassy spot near the birch tree.
He opened the bird guide and gave her
the binoculars: "Choose something
with the naked eye—that dark spot
way up in that birch tree, for example. See it?
Now look at it through the binoculars
and turn the focus wheel." She looked
and focused, and her eyes opened wide,
and her mouth opened wide enough to catch
a starling, if there were any starlings.
But there weren't. There was only
this art. And this artifice.

And years later, after
the divorce, he retrieved his art—
climbed the birch tree again,
his little son waiting in the same
grassy spot where his parents had once
spread a blanket, watching his father now
grow smaller as he rose up in the tree
to take the words back, prying them
from the tattered-wedding-dress-white
arms of the birch tree. And then
he climbed down—*that would be good*
both going and coming back—
and put the words in the little boy's
hands, like a talisman, a creation story
about where he came from—
a favorite poem, a few tangible words
carved in wood, and a murmur
of starlings.

III.

The Thing Is

All the things that can go wrong with a body
could fill a book. Lots of books. A whole medical library.
But the thing is, there's no point in naming them here.
Names that are sometimes long and sometimes short,
sometimes Greek and sometimes Latin. And sometimes
the person who first noticed, studied, and isolated a thing
that went wrong with a body ends up giving his name
to that thing. And thenceforth the people whose bodies
have that thing are given that name for the thing they have.
Which is a nameless thing, really. Nameless as a thousand
dialects of pain. Nevertheless, people are sometimes
made to feel better when given a name for the thing
they have. At least it's a thing, they think. It wasn't just
in their heads. But everything is a thing before it is given
a name. Even the body you have—or, more accurately, *are*—
was a body before it was named. And it goes back to being one.
And that's all that's ever wrong with a body. That's the thing.

PT

She knows the names of all the muscles.
"This here's your supraspinatus,
and this is your infraspinatus,
and here's your teres minor and your
subscapularis," she says, massaging
all around my rotator cuff. I love it when
she talks like that. We've been meeting here
every week for almost a month
and I have a little crush on her. I try my hand
at the new vocabulary: "Is my
subscapularis underneath my scapula?"
"No," she says, "more like in front," then traces
the triangle of it with two very strong index fingers,
and I wince a little. "It actually attaches here
to the anterior surface of your scapula," she says,
"but originates here at the fossa." Her fingers
arrive at the same time that her voice does. I nod
thoughtfully, as if she's telling me something that I can
take home and remember to cherish when
we've gone our separate ways. "It transitions to a tendon
here," she says with a demonstrative jab that hurts
so good. Then, with a long, complicated caress,
she adds, "It inserts itself on the lesser tubercle
of the humerus, in front of the joining capsule. Here."

Gastroenterology

Love is in your colon.
You say *heartache* but it's not
your heart, it's your ascending
and descending colon
absorbing the ups and downs
of your life and all your loves—
the highs pole-vaulting over
your transverse colon,
the deep despairs aching
all the way down in your
rectum. Your colon is you!
And your happiness is
many billions of bacteria
coating your colon and its contents,
living in a healthy balance. Your sadness
is a spastic colon. The intense
feelings your large and small intestines
send up to your brain are
mistranslated as *spiritual, heartfelt,*
dispirited, heartbroken. Even
stomachache is a misnomer: It's all
referred pain and referred joy
from your colon. The referral says
you have a family history. Please
turn on your side and lift your knees.
Let's have a look inside, shall we?

Pain Scale

Doctors aren't good at pain.
They don't know what to do
with the metaphors ("It feels like
a headache in my leg, if that
makes any sense." "It feels like
someone digging around in there
with a hoe, no, sharper: a trowel.")
Or the adjectives ("It's a savage,
ravening pain.") Or the gerunds
("It's a cross between a throbbing
and a stabbing. And a crushing.")
The doctors want numbers: zero
to ten. But the numbers don't do it,
do they? And the doctors don't
know what to do with the people
whose pain cannot be quantified,
only described. Pain for which there
are no numbers, only words. Even
if the words are only: "There are
no words for this, doc—it hurts like
a motherfucker. It's off the scale."

Object Lesson

And what if everything,
everything
I have ever wanted
or will ever want,
is exactly like
this little wooden thing
that I'd forgotten all about
until now, finding it in a box
of my childhood things
that I'm getting rid of because
I don't want them anymore—
this little wooden
toy, this puppet made of wires, wood
and cloth with its round head
and innocent, kissable face,
that I wanted so badly, needed
so terribly that I threw a fit
outside the store
and my mother couldn't
console me, and my father
turned and walked away
from all that foolishness,
all that carrying on,
this little wooden thing
that has found its way back
into my hands now,
so that I hold it up to the light
as if only dimly recognizing
the object of my desire,
smiling to remember it
and shaking my head
the way my father did
when he turned away
from all that foolishness,
all that heartbreak.

Nostalgia

It's pleasant to remember
the house you grew up in,
big as a childhood,
even if it was a small house,
even if it was an unpleasant
childhood, even if
it was an apartment or
just a room you had
to share—still, it is pleasant
to remember the windows,
those little pieces of sky
you could breathe through
just by looking out of them,
which you did as regularly
and unawares as breathing.
Even if there was unhappiness,
even if there was boredom
or pain on the inside, you can
remember those windows now
with pleasure. You can even
count them—go ahead: one
on that side of the bed, two
across from the door, that door
that opened inward from the inside,
the knob on the left, remember?

The Sharpest Knife in the Drawer

He's not, but you know what?
I prefer a wide butter knife myself,
the kind that knows how to spread
the good stuff around, the sort
that slathers it on, gets some on his nose
and chin, then wipes it dopily on his sleeve.

The sharp ones put me on edge.
They make me uncomfortable.
And anyway, they don't live in the drawer—
they live up there on the other side
of the countertop, their perfect teeth
hidden in the wooden slots. Bottom

line: I love a long-handled ice cream spoon,
the kind that knows how to plumb
the depths of the tapered sundae glass
for the last drop of fudge.

Premature Ejaculation

"I love you," he blurted on their second date
before they'd placed their order,
before he knew anything about her—
her middle name, her place in the order
of her siblings, her favorite color, season, author, aria,
breakfast food, ice cream flavor, the name
of her cat, the name of her alma mater.

"You don't even know me," she said, feeling
more alarmed than flattered, folding
and unfolding her napkin while he looked
down at his lap, as though that's where
all his overzealousness had spilled out,
spoiling everything, the gum-chewing
waitress flipping her pad open, licking her pencil.

Poem to Be Read at 3AM

When I wake up at 3AM to pee,
I like to think of all the other people
waking up at 3AM to pee
like me—the sounds of all the toilets
flushing, then slowly filling up again
as we trudge through the inscrutable darkness
back to bed, tossing and turning
and thinking we're the only ones
sleep has forsaken. And I like to think
about the expression "toss and turn"
while I'm tossing and turning, and about the first
anonymous person who said it that way,
and all the people who know what it means
to toss and turn because they've tossed
and turned themselves, and are maybe doing it
right now with me. Well, not *with* me—
we're doing it separately. But somehow
we're doing it together. And when I think of that,
it makes me feel less alone, if you know
what I mean. Which somehow I think you do.

Riddle

It could kill you
or it could kiss you
so glancingly
that you don't feel a thing
and you give it
to someone you love
like a kiss
of death without
knowing it.
You can't see it
but those who know
say it looks like
the pearl-and-diamond
tiaras of ancient monarchs
who commanded armies
in wars that lasted years
and killed millions.

Face Mask

Have you noticed
how beautiful
everyone looks

when all you can see
are their eyes?
Something about

the imagination,
how it conjures
a perfectly

beautiful face
in the eyes
of the beholder

facing a pandemic
and a polity
with so many unveiled

ugly hatreds.

The News

"There was no news today,"
said the anchor
on the 6 o'clock news,
then she quietly laid down her pen,
removed her audio feed,
and smiling a truly
sad smile, stood up and
gracefully walked off the set.
And though the people
were still suffering and dying
and killing each other off
all over the world, the world itself
still dying, our leaders
leading us over its proverbial edge;
though greed was still masquerading
as good and love was still
greater than fear—even though fear
was still mostly winning out—
today none of it was news.
Because it was the same as yesterday.
And yesterday was the same
as the other yesterdays, which somehow,
incredibly, was news today. The news
was that there was no news.
And it was big news. Real news.

Non, Je Ne Regrette Rien

Not even that nasty thing
you said to Grace Labiner in the 6th grade
for no other reason than you liked her
and didn't know what to do
with your feelings? That was *tres relou*
of you. Or when you stopped talking
to Arnold DiGiorgio, your best friend
since kindergarten, just because your new
JV friends said he was a fairy? That was
impardonnable. And what about that little
fire you technically started, the one that grew
into something pyrotechnically
irrevocable and criminal? That was totally *fou*
of you. And don't forget that despicable
taunt you spat at your mother, who
loved everything French—especially Edith Piaf—
and only wanted you to love it, too. The truth is,
people who say they regret nothing
are either lying or in denial or flying blind. Even Piaf—
who, when she heard Monsieur Dumont
play that song on the piano in her living room
for the first time, cried out "*Formidable,*
I must have it for my performance at *L'Olympia*"—
had just that morning been quite rude
to the composer, making him wait a whole hour
before she appeared—furious, curt, and in a bad mood.
"OK," she growled, "One song, hurry up, play it"—
because she disliked him and didn't want to grant him
an audition. But she adored his new song,
which eventually became her biggest hit
and an anthem of the French Foreign Legion.
And if she said she didn't regret
treating him shabbily that morning, *bien alors,*
she was full of shit.

Agape

First you notice the sound
of the woman singing
on the subway platform,

then you notice that she isn't
very good—in fact, she's
tone-deaf, God love her—

belting it out among
the waiting passengers
as the approaching train

begins to drown her out
with the roar of its engine,
so that her wide-open mouth

and her wide-open eyes
look less like song than
wonder and surprise

as you bend your knee
to gently lay your dollar bill
into her empty cup,

God love her.

Good Cry

I hadn't had one in years. I was
due. But the question was
where to have it, where to
do it? "You could do it here,"
said my therapist, taking in the tasteful
prints on the wall, the braided rug,
the upholstered sofa and chairs
with a wave of her upturned hand.
But that would feel like taking a dump
in the middle of your office, I thought
but did not say. "No," I said, "I have to do it
alone." "But that defeats the purpose—
a good cry is better when shared," she said.
We both looked out the window
at the gray day, the constipated sky.
There was a long silence. I could feel her
checking the time. It started to rain,
then changed its mind. "Our time
is up," she said. So I went and sat in my car
and did it. And the people passed by
beneath their umbrellas. And the sidewalk
moaned. And the streetlights flickered.
I felt cleansed. I felt wrung. That night,
when I told my wife about it, she said,
a little ruefully, that she wished it was something
we could have done together. And she wept a little.
And I wept a little with her, which felt good.
But the one in the car was better.

Great Tits

Some would say
it's not OK to say,
much less write,
not to mention title
your poem the thing
you're thinking
when you're thinking
what I'm thinking
about the thing itself,
the things themselves,
because focusing on them,
objectively speaking,
objectifies and sexualizes.
And yet, subjectively
speaking, historically
speaking, they have
inspired great things from great
poets, artists, kings,
not to mention chemists;
the word *sublimate*
comes to mind—the way a thing
or things pass from
solid to gaseous phase,
such as ice changing
into water vapor
in air or the perfectly
lovely body of a woman
passing into memory
or imagination—the effect
may be seen in winter
above snowfields
when the sun is out.

Chamber Pot

When first they learned about Paul Revere
in their 6th grade classroom—his famous ride,
the advancing British troops, the Longfellow poem
("One, if by land, two, if by sea") they were
unimpressed. And now on the field trip
to Boston's North End, crowded together inside
the tiny 300-year-old Paul Revere House,
the docent pointing out the original hearth,
wainscot, beams and ceiling joists, they are still
unimpressed. Then, out of nowhere, a chamber pot
changes everything: One of the children notices it
under the four-poster, raises his hand, and asks
what it is. "A chamber pot," says the docent. "For pooping
and peeing." Titters, gasps, giggles and groans go up,
and up go the hands, the follow-up questions buzzing
around the master bedroom of Paul and Sarah Revere,
the children more interested now than they ever were
in any part of the patriot's story or the country's.
"Didn't they have bathrooms?" "What about
toilet paper?" "What about privacy?" "What about
the smell?" "Where did they empty it?" The class
is all ears now, and the docent is hitting her stride
because this is interesting stuff, this is important historical
stuff: "Bathrooms were invented much later," she says,
"in the 19th century. Here it was either the chamber pot
or a long cold walk to the outhouse in the middle
of the night. They emptied them in the street—everyone did.
They didn't know about hygiene. They didn't yet know
about germ theory. The smell was hideous. People got sick.
They died young. Paul Revere had sixteen children,
but only nine survived." And now the class is learning.
They're rapt. Engaged. Impressed! And all because poops
and pees are basic. The stuff of life, of history. The stuff of poetry.

Authorized

The sign at the end of the corridor
says *Authorized Personnel Only.*

"Are you authorized?" he says.
"I'm an author," I say. "I have
authored. I am authorial."

"Don't be smart," he says.
"I'm not smart," I say. "I'm
pretty average, really. A writer
writes. Period. And reads a lot."

"You can't be here," he says,
his finger worrying his holster.

"There is no verb *to be,*" I say,
"in American Sign Language.
Which doesn't mean that Deaf
Americans aren't. Or that they don't
talk about being." And I hold up
one forefinger.

"I'm going to count to three," he says.
And he holds up one forefinger.

"Your forefinger and my forefinger," I say,
"are two persons, two personnel,
two pronouns, two classifiers
in ASL."

"Two," he says.

"But that's classified," I say,
hoping it might disarm him.

"Three," he says,
and I blow him a kiss.

“Breaker 1-9,” he says into his walkie-talkie,
staring straight at me. “We’ve got
a nut job here. Do you copy?”

That’s when I take out my hand-turned
red cedar pen, and I begin copying
this all down.

IV.

ASL Crown

1.

Maybe I should tell the ending first.
In the beginning was the ending.
If it's a story worth telling, a song
worth singing, it should sing itself. KISS-FIST
is one sign for love. Two fists crossed
at the chest, like a hug, is another. Signing
was hands-down the most beautiful singing
I had ever seen in my life. That's the gist
of the story, the plot, the characters, each
and every visual rhyme, first line to last.
When you fall in love with a language, you fall
in love with the people who call that language
home. One day, I took a sign language class,
and I ended up marrying the teacher.

2.

I married my sign language teacher.
But I never got higher than a B minus
because my receptive skills sucked. Plus,
I wasn't able to master the classifiers,
which are pronouns, those basic features
of ASL that we hearing people mess
up most: Bodies moving through space.
I also sucked at face. And facial grammar.
But I was good at tongue: able to impress
with my adverbs, which got her saying YES
YES YES. And KISS-FIST on our third date.
The verb of us. I asked her to conjugate it
in the future perfect. It was an interfaith wedding,
a lesbian rabbi and Methodist preacher presiding.

3.

The lesbian rabbi and Methodist minister
stood beside me underneath the chuppah
waiting for the bride, who was late. DEAF-PUH,
quipped a Deaf guest in a signed whisper
to another Deaf guest, causing a snicker,
then a knee-slapping giggle. "The chutzpah,"
growled Uncle Hank, adjusting his kippah,
glaring at the juggling hands. He winced or
ducked each time a hand flitted or darted
from a sleeve. Finally, when the piano and cello
began fingering Pachelbel's Canon in D,
my blushing Deaf bride glided in, diffidently
avoiding my eyes. One of the Deaf guests farted.
A bad sign. Star-crossed lovers from the get-go.

4.

We were star-crossed lovers from the get-go:
Ninety percent of mixed marriages (Deaf
and Hearing) fail. A spoonerism: "Death
Man Found Frozen to Deaf in Snow."
A misnomer: "Deaf-mute." A palindrome:
The-fingers-of-both-my-hands-pleading-with
her-to-reconsider-palms-up-in-the-air (left
to right, right to left: same). A synecdoche:
"My pleas fell on deaf ears." We divorced
after 7 years. Just another statistic. And the worst
part was: "Visitation" (a son and a daughter—
beautiful boy, Hearing; beautiful girl, Deaf):
"Alternate weekends." I saw them less than half
their childhood. A platitude: "Nothing lasts forever."

5.

Nothing lasts forever: The platitude she signed
blithely with a thumb-and-pinky flourish. Calumny:
the gossip swirling around the Deaf community
from hand to hand, whispered indictments behind
my back, the unheard and unanswerable kind.
She sued for full custody. Child support and alimony.
I got them every other weekend, plus Wednesday
nights for dinner and homework. Back to Mom's by 9.
Her head poked out the front door like a tightly wound
cuckoo in a clock. Check and release, cogs with teeth,
minute hand, second hand, conditions, strictures,
lawyers, and more lawyers. Divorce is a death
with no rattle. No last breath. No discernible sound.
Two beautiful children. Here, I have pictures.

6.

Two beautiful children. Here, I have photos—
Oops, I still reach for my wallet out of habit
though the pix are in my phone. I hate
these smartphones, truly. But I love the video
apps—FaceTime, Glide, and MarcPolo—
for phoning my daughter in ASL. A bit
freaky, isn't it, signing to a satellite—
which must be where the signs all go. Roll over,
Alexander Graham Bell! You and Beethoven
both! Signing is the most beautiful singing
the world has ever seen. This is a picture
of my son: He has my forehead, my aquiline
nose. My daughter has her mother's coloring.
Both kids have her hands, her best feature.

7.

They have their mother's hands, her best feature.
My daughter has my hand eczema. And my
weltschmerz. Systemic conditions both. Try
aloe. Try not watching the news so much or
at all. Try a vegan diet. Try reading more fiction.
Both kids are athletic, which they got from me.
And they sign fluently, my daughter gracefully,
my son lazily, as though he were a dictionary
of one-handed signs. "The boy signs like a one-
armed bandit," I complained to his mother
when I dropped the kids off. "He's your son,"
she parried. "He got it from you." Then added,
"He also got your Attention Deficit Disorder."
Visitations are for angels and divorced dads.

8.

Visitations are for angels and divorced dads
bearing pepperoni pizzas cooling in boxes.
I made them the best lunches. Bagels, lox and
cream cheese, Thanksgiving sandwiches, scads
of gummy bears. Packed them in lunch bags,
the padded, insulated, leak-proof kind (Red Sox-
emblazoned), placed lovingly in their backpacks
every other Monday morning, when I had
them. When I had another chance to make
it right. Which I don't think I ever did. *I'm sorry.*
No ideas but in things: A lunch box can still
choke me up. Spontaneous overflow of powerful
feelings. Feelings I don't think I named. *I'm sorry.*
Maybe a poem is the right thing to say too late.

9.

Maybe a poem is the right thing to say too late,
years later, a lifetime later. If an apology
falls from your lips and there is nobody
there to hear it, does it make a sound? If you make
the sign with your hand, stirring the A handshape
clockwise over your heart—excruciatingly
heartfelt—and there is nobody there to see it,
is it still a speech act? Is it done by being stated?
A poem is the best words in their best order,
spoken or signed. SORRY and STORY in ASL
don't rhyme. SORRY rhymes with ULTRASOUND
and MOSQUITO. Visual rhyme. DEAF is a noun.
HEARING occurs at the mouth. I was one syllable
short of sorry. I never said *I'm sorry.* I said *I'm sore.*

10.

I never did say *I'm sorry.* I said *I'm*
sore. I hurt. I hate. Your fault. And the f-word
as grammatical ejaculation, adjective, adverb,
and especially imperative. The f-word rhymes
with *truck,* which my son, around that time,
couldn't pronounce: The initial consonant cluster *tr*
eluded him. He loved trucks, though. "Look," he cheered
whenever he saw one, "a fuck!" His *fucks* and mine
rang out like bicycle bells (his) and pneumatic air horns
on tractor trailers (mine), mixing in the charged air
around our imploded family. I blamed her for it—
she dropped the ball, she dropped the bomb,
the IED. Though I didn't turn the kids against her,
I dropped hints. It was the best I could do at the time.

11.

The best I could do at the time was not get drunk
to drown out the pain. I had a good excuse
to unplug the jug. I had grounds. I had a bruised
ego, broken heart, child support and alimony—a chunk
of change. Plus lawyer fees. My bottom line sank
like the mercury in the thermostat. The pipes froze.
The For Sale sign dangled out front like a loose
tooth, abscessed, half-extracted. It all stunk
of infection. Who wouldn't drink? I sat for a long
time at the intersection, thinking. No blinker:
Turn right, to the bar, drink myself into oblivion.
Turn left, to the Twelve Step meeting. Step One:
Life is unmanageable. A car behind me honked.
All I could see was my own bruised longing.

12.

All I could see was my own bruised longing
for a long, long time. “Would you rather be right
or have peace?” my sponsor asked. The Eighth
Step: Made a list of people we’d harmed. Willing
to make amends to them all. Point your finger
at anyone, and three fingers point back. RIGHT
is a pointing right hand pounding a left one like
a pile driver. It’ll drive you into the ground, singing
“I’m right” all the way down. The sign PEACE,
on the other hand, is a soft hand-clasp made twice,
then the pronated palms gently falling like leaves
in autumn, a kind of deciduous sign, a hyphenated
compound sign. SORRY is a full declarative
sentence. The subject “I” is understood, elided.

13.

The "I" is understood, elided, the subject
missing in action, the person of interest
disinterested at best, absent at worst,
which was his alibi: He couldn't be a suspect
if he wasn't there. He was elsewhere. In fact,
he was in his head, in the poem. He was lost
in his imagination. Checked out. His chest
hurts. It pricks. What's he doing? He's in the act
of saying something, signing something. What
does it mean that his closed fist begins
doing these 360s over his heart, turning and
turning like a figure skater twirling around
and around, performing these heartfelt spins
without beginning or end, clockwise as fate?

14.

No beginning or end, clockwise as fate,
this circle, this sign for making amends.
But SORRY doesn't really count as amends.
It doesn't recompense, doesn't compensate
for the loss, the injury, the wrongdoing. Wait—
wrongdoing? But there was no fault, no grounds
for divorce. There was only the ground
fault, the electrical current that somehow strayed
and stopped flowing between us. Suddenly
it flowed directly into the earth, into the ground,
and the circuit went dead, the light went out
in her eyes. Then in my eyes. It was even gone
in the kids' eyes for a time (and for *that* I'm sorry),
flickering, blinking—but then it came back on.

15.

The ending was in the beginning: First,
I ended up marrying my sign language teacher.
There was a lesbian rabbi and a Lutheran preacher.
Second, all signs said the marriage was star-crossed.
Third, I ended up with a platitude (*Nothing lasts*
forever) and two beautiful children. Look, pictures:
They have their mother's hands, her best feature.
Visitations are for angels and divorced
dads. A poem is the right thing to say too late.
I don't think I ever said *I'm sorry.* I said *I'm sore,*
which I guess was the best I could do at the time,
drunk as I was on my own bruised longing. SORRY
is a full sentence—the "I" understood, elided—
circular, no beginning or end, clockwise as fate.

Acknowledgments

Thanks to the following publications in which these poems, or earlier versions of them, first appeared:

Aji: "The Thing Is"
Galleywinter: "Trump Inaugural Poem"
Glimpse: "Hold at the Circulation Desk," "Going Back"
Hawaii Pacific Review: "Barbershop"
Journal of Compressed Literature: "To a Toddler Bawling in a Pram"
Leaping Clear: "Cat Poem," "Good Book"
Literary Accents: "Birches," "Premature Ejaculation"
Mad Swirl: "Poem at the Breakfast Place," "Recycled Sestina"
Medical Literary Messenger: "Gastroenterology"
Necessary Fiction: "Anonymity"
New Verse News: "No News"
Red Planet Review: "Object Lesson," "Omission"
Sein und Werden: "To the One Who Stole a Book at My Poetry Reading"
Solstice: "Vernal Scrooge"
Spillway: "That She's Beautiful"
Under a Warm Green Linden: "Love Letter to Carl Sandburg"
Upstreet: "Talent"
Vox Populi: "Wording"
Wordgathering: "Authorized"

About FutureCycle Press

FutureCycle Press is dedicated to publishing lasting English-language poetry in both print-on-demand and Kindle formats. Founded in 2007 by long-time independent editor/publishers and partners Diane Kistner and Robert S. King, the press incorporated as a nonprofit in 2012. A number of our editors are distinguished poets and writers in their own right, and we have been actively involved in the small press movement going back to the early seventies.

We award the FutureCycle Poetry Book Prize and honorarium annually for the best full-length volume of poetry we published that year. Introduced in 2013, proceeds from our Good Works projects are donated to charity. Our Selected Poems series highlights contemporary poets with a substantial body of work to their credit; with this series we strive to resurrect work that has had limited distribution and is now out of print.

We are dedicated to giving all of the authors we publish the care their work deserves, offering a catalog of the most diverse and distinguished work possible, and paying forward any earnings to fund more great books. All of our books are kept "alive" and available unless and until an author requests a title be taken out of print.

We've learned a few things about independent publishing over the years. We've also evolved a unique and resilient publishing model that allows us to focus mainly on vetting and preserving for posterity poetry collections of exceptional quality without becoming overwhelmed with bookkeeping and mailing, fundraising activities, or taxing editorial and production "bubbles." To find out more about what we are doing, come see us at www.futurecycle.org.

The FutureCycle Poetry Book Prize

All full-length poetry books published by FutureCycle Press in a given calendar year are considered for the annual FutureCycle Poetry Book Prize. This allows us to consider each submission on its own merits, outside of the context of a traditional contest. Too, the judges see the finished book, which will have benefitted from the beautiful book design and strong editorial gloss we are famous for.

The book ranked the best in judging is announced as the prize-winner in the subsequent year. There is no fixed monetary award; instead, the winning poet receives an honorarium of 20% of the total net royalties from all poetry books and chapbooks the press sold online in the year the winning book was published. The winner is also accorded the honor of being on the panel of judges for the next year's competition; all judges receive copies of all contending books to keep for their personal library.

www.ingramcontent.com/pod-product-compliance
Lightning Source LLC
LaVergne TN
LVHW020049110826
845155LV00029B/696

* 9 7 8 1 9 5 2 5 9 3 1 7 8 *